BRAZILIAN
BRACELETS

Sandra Lebrun

SEARCH PRESS

Contents

Materials

Beads, wooden toggles, buttons or bells for finishing off

A pair of scissors

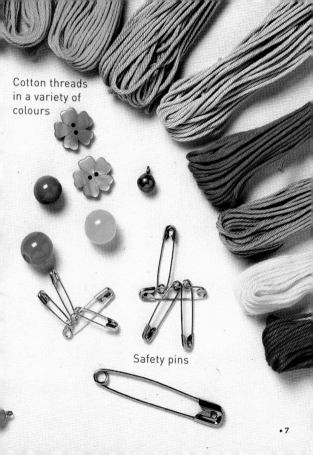

Cotton threads in a variety of colours

Safety pins

Friendship bracelets

These bracelets are bursting with vibrant colour and excitement, reflecting the festive culture of their Brazilian homeland. In recent times, young backpackers would return from Brazil with these cotton bracelets as presents for their friends, and it was their parents who gave them the affectionate nickname 'friendship bracelets'.

The Brazilian tradition is to make a wish as you tie the bracelet round your wrist – and then never take it off. Fortunately, as they are made from cotton yarn, you can wear your bracelet all the time, even when showering, while playing sport or swimming.

With time, the thread will slowly wear through until your lucky charm eventually falls off. It is then that your wish will come true ...

The key is to experiment with colours. Whether you prefer an understated look or a more zany one; or whether you wish to use stripes, spots or herringbone patterns, take your time to make your friendship bracelets unique. Either keep them for yourself or give them to friends and family. Children and adults alike will appreciate these fun and thoughtful gifts.

Sandra Lebrun

Starting your bracelet

Start by securing the end of your bracelet with a firm knot. There are several ways of doing this.

The knot
Knot all the strands together at one end and start your bracelet directly. Leave a 10cm (4in) strand if you want to make this end into a braid.

The simple loop
Bunch all the threads together, make a loop at one end and tie a knot to secure the loop in place. You can cut off any bits of thread that are too long. If you want to braid this end of the loop, use 10cm (4in) of thread.

The double loop

Fold your thread in half lengthways and make a loop in the middle held in place with a knot.

If you use this loop you must remember that with two threads you will get four threads for the bracelet. If you need four 70cm (27½in) threads, double the length and use two 140cm (55in) threads.

You can hold the threads in place by attaching them to your trouser leg using a safety pin. This will anchor your threads for you to begin weaving.

Finishing off your bracelet

There are several different methods to choose from, depending on how you want to tie the bracelet onto your wrist.

The knot
To finish off your bracelet, you can simply bunch the threads together and tie them in a knot.

The bead
Once you have reached the length you require, thread the strands through the bead, tie them in a knot and cut off any remaining thread.

If you started with a loop, you can pop the bead through the loop to do it up. Make sure the bead is big enough not to slip back through the loop.

The braid

Once you have reached the length you require, braid the threads for about 4cm (1½in) more. Finish with a knot. It doesn't matter if you aren't using a number of threads that is divisible by three; separate the threads, for example, into three groups of one strand, two strands and one strand.

If you started the bracelet with a knot or a simple loop, you can undo this and make the threads into a braid. This will then give you two ties for attaching your bracelet.

The basic knots

You must always hold the thread(s) in position with your left hand, pulling the threads towards you: this hand acts as the frame. Use your right hand to work the threads.

To start, imagine that the threads are numbered 1, 2, 3, etc. from left to right.

Terminology

A 'right knot' means a knot that loops the thread to the right of the bracelet. And a 'left knot' means a knot that sends the thread to the left of the bracelet.

Right knot

Pull thread 2 taut with your left hand. Take thread 1 in your right hand, pass it over thread 2, then back under and bring it through the loop from back to front. Pull on the threads to tighten and you have your first right knot.

Left knot

Pull thread 1 taut with your left hand. Take thread 2 in your right hand, pass it over thread 1, then back under and bring it through the loop from back to front. Pull on the threads to tighten and you have your first left knot.

Wrapping

With your left hand pull all the threads towards you. Use your left index finger to support the core threads as you wrap the outer thread(s) round the others, holding the outer thread(s) in place each time.

Knotting and wrapping techniques

The difference between Brazilian and wrap bracelets simply depends on whether you use a knotting or wrapping technique.

Brazilian bracelets

This style consists of a series of knots. For the simple model (see page 34) and for the herringbone model (see page 40), remember that you always need two knots, one on top of the other.

Make the first knot and pull it tight, then make a second identical knot using the same threads and pull it tight on top of the first. Thread 1, which was on the left, has now moved to the right and can be knotted with thread 3 using two knots one after the other, and so on.

When a line is finished, start again from the left using thread 2, moving it across to the right, then repeat with thread 3.

Wrap bracelets

• You don't have to stick to using cotton thread. Have fun mixing materials: leather, glitter thread, narrow ribbons, etc.
• Choose the order of colours by testing them first against a piece of paper. It is best to have an idea of your pattern before starting.
• To start, you will need a number of threads, each 70cm (27½in) long. Don't forget that if you are starting with a knot in the middle of the length, you will need strands that are 140cm (55in) long.
• As you are wrapping the thread round, make sure the wraps don't overlap.
• If you think there is too much of a gap between any of the wraps, you can push them together so that they bunch up more neatly.
• Use your left index finger to hold the wrapping in place.
• When you want to stop wrapping, take the thread and make a right knot by pulling it through the loop formed by the last turn.

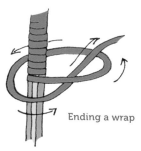

Ending a wrap

The simple wrap

One thread wraps round all the others and in a flick of the wrist your bracelet takes shape!

> Materials
> 4 cotton threads each 70cm (27½in) long
> in green, yellow, pink and orange

On each turn, your left index finger will hold the wrapping thread in place as it passes round the core threads (see page 15).

1 With your left hand, hold all the threads taut
towards you. Use your left index finger to hold the
thread in place as you wrap it round the core threads,
passing it to the left-hand side. Manoeuvre the thread
with your right hand to complete the wrap. Your left
index finger holds each turn of the thread in place so
that it doesn't come undone.

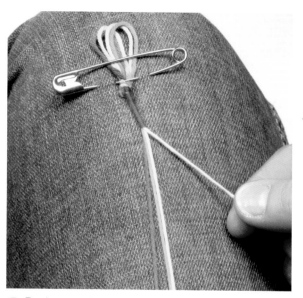

2 To change colour, end the current wrapping with the thread on the left-hand side and hold it taut with the other threads. With your right hand, select another colour and start wrapping it round the core strands again.

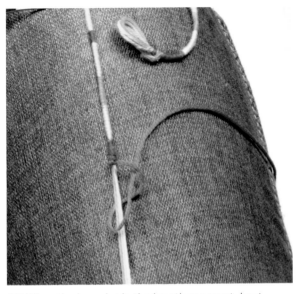

3 When the bracelet is the length you want, knot the thread on the right, then thread on a bead, followed by a knot (see page 12).

The striped wrap

Now you have mastered the wrapping technique, have fun playing with colours!

> Materials
> 4 cotton threads each 70cm (27½in) long in orange, lime green, red and yellow

Use your left index finger to hold the threads securely in place as you wrap (see pages 15 and 17).

1 As with the simple wrap, when you want to change colour, end the current wrapping with the thread to the left and hold it tout with the other threads. Using your right hand, choose two other colours and start wrapping them round the core strands again.

2 Wrap the two threads round side by side,
creating a striped pattern; end on the left-hand
side when you have completed a sufficient length
in that colour combination. Place them with the
other threads and continue in another colour.

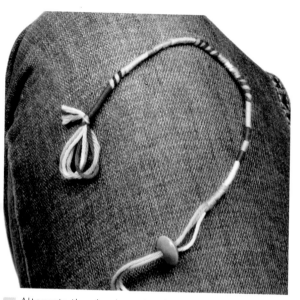

3 Alternate the simple and striped wraps until your bracelet is the right length. Finish the last turn with a knot, thread on a bead and tie all the threads together (see page 12).

Fine bracelet

This easy, understated bracelet takes only a few minutes to make and can be worn on its own or with several others.

> Materials
> 2 cotton threads each 70cm (27½in) long in grey and blue

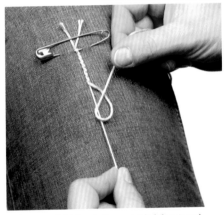

Make one right knot, then one left knot and continue in the same way until you reach the length you want. One colour is always knotted to the right and the other colour is always knotted to the left.

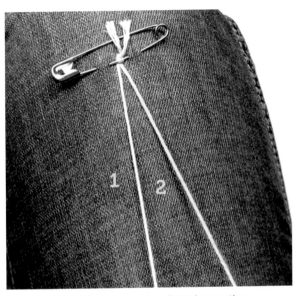

1 Make a knot to tie your two threads together.

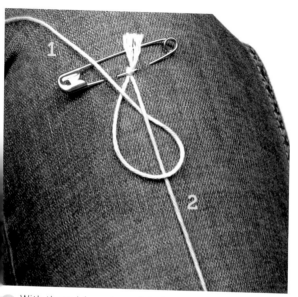

With thread 1, make a right knot. Return your threads to the step 1 position.

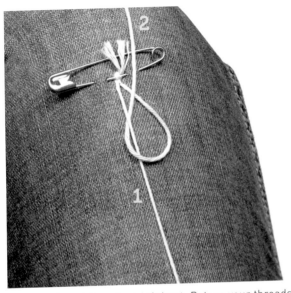

3 With thread 2, make a left knot. Return your threads to the step 1 position.

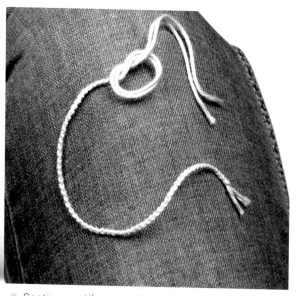

4 Continue until you reach the length you want and finish off the bracelet as you began it by knotting the two threads together.

Simple Brazilian bracelet

These bracelets are made using a series of double knots.

Materials
4 cotton threads each 90cm
(35½in) long in purple, mauve,
pink and pale pink

Start with a simple loop. Remember that you always need two knots, one on top of the other. Make an initial knot, pull tight, then make a second identical one using the same threads pulled tight on top of the first (see page 16).

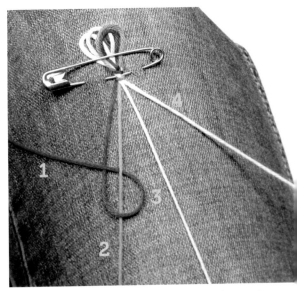

1 Arrange the threads in your chosen colour order. Using thread 1, make a right knot over thread 2. Pull tight. Using thread 1, make another right knot over thread 2.

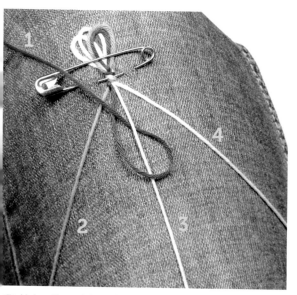

Using thread 1, make a right knot over thread 3.
Pull tight and make a second identical knot. Repeat
with thread 1 over thread 4.

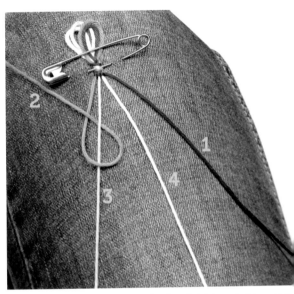

3 When thread 1 reaches the far right-hand side, start the same process with thread 2: two right knots over thread 3, two knots over thread 4 and two knots over thread 1. Thread 2 is now to the right of the bracelet.

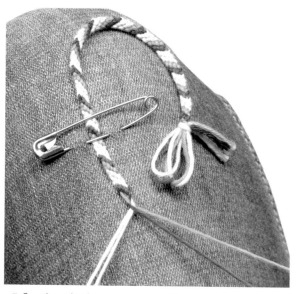

4 Continue in the same way until you reach the desired length and finish the bracelet with a braid and then a knot.

Brazilian herringbone bracelet

There are many combinations you can try. Remember to consider the order of your threads before you start.

Materials
8 cotton threads each 90cm (35½in) long in purple, green and mauve

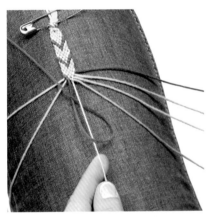

Once again this uses the double-knot principle (see page 16). Use your left hand to hold taut the strand that you are tying the knot round. The purple thread makes a right knot, followed by another one to finish the first half of the V shape.

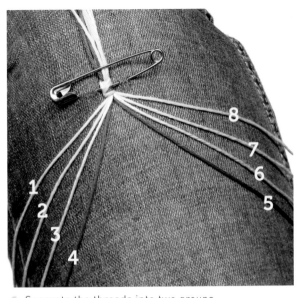

1 Separate the threads into two groups.

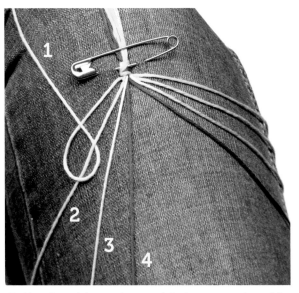

2 Use thread 1 to make two right knots over thread 2, then two right knots over thread 3, then two right knots over thread 4. Stop there.

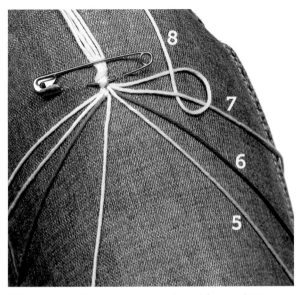

3 On the right-hand side, use thread 8 to make two left knots over thread 7, two left knots over thread 6, then two left knots over thread 5. Stop there.

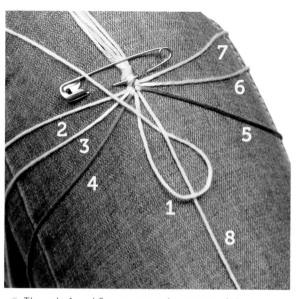

4 Threads 1 and 8 are now at the centre of the two groups. Using thread 1, make two right knots over thread 8.

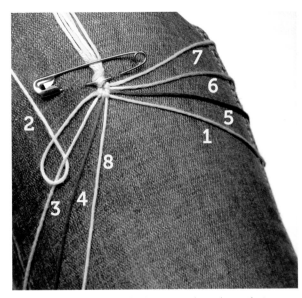

5 Now start again with the outer threads so that threads 2 and 7 meet in the centre. Then, using thread 2, make two right knots over thread 7. Repeat the entire procedure until you reach the length you want.

6 Finish with a braid and a knot. Undo the starting knot and braid the strands together so that both ends match.

Polka-dot bracelet

The metallic thread gives this bracelet a touch of elegance and also helps it to hold its shape better.

Materials

10 cotton threads, including 6 black 100cm (39½in) long and 4 metallic grey 90cm (35½in) long

If you start with a loop, five threads will suffice, as long as the threads are folded double so there are ten strands for weaving. The metallic grey threads are in the centre. The black threads will meet in the middle under the silver diamond shapes, then move to the sides under the silver spots.

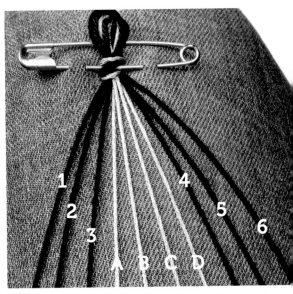

1 Arrange the black threads on the outside and the silver threads in the centre. Start by using threads A, B, C and D.

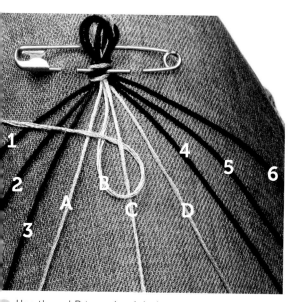

2 Use thread B to make right knots round threads C and D. Then use thread A to make right knots round threads C and D. This gives you a diamond shape.

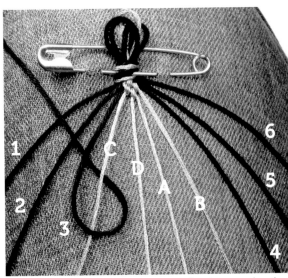

3 All the black threads are now going to go under the diamond with thread 3, make right knots round threads C and D. Then with thread 4, make left knots round threads B and A. These two black threads are now in the centre.

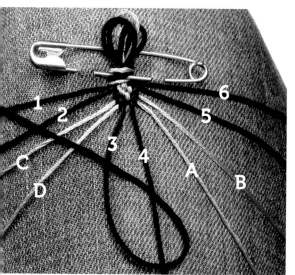

4 Threads 3 and 4 are directly underneath the diamond. With thread 3 make a double right knot around thread 4. Thread 3 will now be to the right of thread 4. Repeat step 3 with threads 2 and 5. They meet up again between threads 4 and 3 and are attached by using thread 2 to make a double right knot over thread 5. Repeat with threads 1 and 6, which meet up again in the centre between threads 5 and 2. Using thread 1, make a double right knot over thread 6. Thread 1 is now to the right of thread 6.

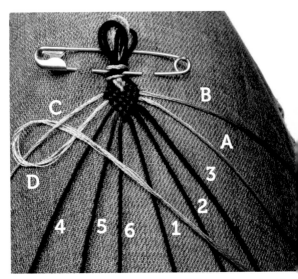

5 For the silver spots, use thread D to make a double left knot round thread C. Then use thread A to make a double right knot round thread B. Once the spots are finished, all the black threads will separate into two groups to pass to the outside edges of the bracelet, under the dots.

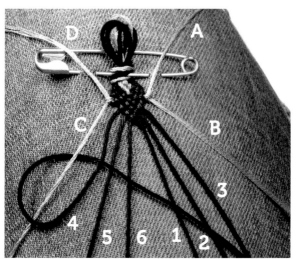

6 With thread 4, make left knots round threads C and D.
With thread 5 do the same round threads C, D and 4. Use
thread 6 to do the same again round threads C, D, 4 and 5.
Work in the same from the right. With thread 3, make right
knots round threads B and A. With thread 2 do the same
round threads B, A and 3. Thread 1 does the same again
round threads B, A, 3 and 2. All the threads will now be back
in their starting position Start again from Step 1 until you
reach the length you want. You can then finish off with
a braid at each end.

Zigzag

Using red and vanilla threads, this design is easier than you think.

Materials
5 cotton threads each
140cm (55in) long in
strawberry, cherry,
blackcurrant,
raspberry and vanilla

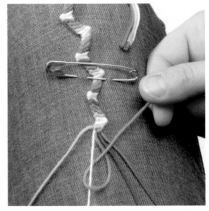

The threads are knotted one by one to the right and when you reach the end with the vanilla thread, you turn back and knot them all to the left.

1 To start, make a loop that you will undo at the end and braid. Arrange the threads in your chosen colour order.

2 Using thread 1, make right knots round threads 2, 3, 4 and then 5. Do the same again with thread 2 round threads 3, 4, 5 and 1. Knot thread 3 round threads 4, 5, 1 and 2. Knot thread 4 round threads 5, 1, 2 and 3.

3 Using thread 5, make right knots round threads 1, 2, 3 and 4. When you reach the end, thread 5 does an about turn to go back again. Still using thread 5, make a series of left knots round threads 4, 3, 2 and 1.

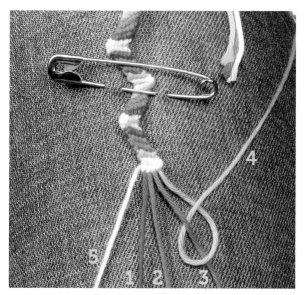

4 Now it's thread 4's turn to be knotted to the left round threads 3, 2, 1 and 5. Then knot thread 3 back round threads 2, 1, 5 and 4. Knot thread 2 round threads 1, 5, 4 and 3. Knot thread 1 round threads 5, 4, 3 and 2. You are then back to your starting position. Repeat until you reach the length you want and finish with a braid at both ends.

First published in Great Britiain in 2015 by
Search Press Ltd.
Wellwood, North Farm Road,
Tunbridge Wells,
Kent, TN2 3DR

© Larousse 2013
Original French title published as *Bracelets brésiliens*

English translation by Burravoe Translation Services

Typesetting by Greengate Publishing Services, Tonbridge, Kent

ISBN: 978-1-78221-242-3

Photographs: Olivier Ploton
Styling: Sandra Lebrun
Photography credit : IGS-CP

Printed in China